M000160243

THE LITTLE BOOK OF
# CAMPING

Published in 2022 by OH!
An Imprint of Welbeck Non-Fiction Limited,
part of Welbeck Publishing Group.
Based in London and Sydney.
www.welbeckpublishing.com

**Disclaimer:**
This book is intended for general informational purposes only and should not be relied upon as recommending or promoting any specific practice, diet or method of treatment. It is not intended to diagnose, advise, treat or prevent any illness or condition and is not a substitute for advice from a professional practitioner of the subject matter contained in this book. You should not use the information in this book as a substitute for medication, nutritional, diet, spiritual or other treatment that is prescribed by your practitioner. The publisher makes no representations or warranties with respect to the accuracy, completeness or currency of the contents of this work, and specifically disclaim, without limitation, any implied warranties of merchantability or fitness for a particular purpose and any injury, illness, damage, death, liability or loss incurred, directly or indirectly from the use or application of any of the contents of this book. Furthermore, the publisher is not affiliated with and does not sponsor or endorse any uses of or beliefs about in any way referred in this book.

ISBN 978-1-80069-183-4

Compiled and written by: Malcolm Croft
Editorial: Lisa Dyer
Project manager: Russell Porter
Design: Tony Seddon
Production: Rachel Burgess

A CIP catalogue record for this book is available from the British Library

Printed in China

10 9 8 7 6 5 4 3 2 1

# THE LITTLE BOOK OF
# CAMPING

## PERFECTLY PITCHED WIT
## & WISDOM FOR AN OUTDOOR
## ADVENTURE

# CONTENTS

# INTRODUCTION

That glug of cold beer on a hot sunny day after a long day of hiking. The snap, crackle and pop of a roaring campfire. The smell of a caramelized marshmallow. That rush of blood to the head from successfully pitching your tent. That feeling of needing to wee but too scared to leave your tent. That dread from the eerie noise you heard in the dead of night. The terrible night's sleep.

Ah, yes, we must be camping!

After the lockdowns, social restrictions and bouts of stay-at-home self-isolation in recent history, it was no surprise to anyone that camping outside away from other human beings became more popular than ever before. The focus on climate change and a planet under threat from industrialization also served to remind us of our essential connection with the great outdoors. Camping is the clarion call we all – yes, you – needed to return home to nature, reclaim our roots, get back to basics, become one with the birds, bees and bears, and recharge our batteries. (Don't forget to pack spare batteries.) More people – of all shapes and sizes, from all counties and countries – today seek refuge in the warm embrace of Mother Nature's pillowy bosom. Like chicken soup, camping is good for the soul, despite how ridiculous it may feel to leave a perfectly warm home with solid walls to sleep on the ground in the cold next to all manner of wildlife ready to nibble you. But that's what camping is all about – living with the wild – searching the stars above, connecting to the earth below, enveloping all your senses in the world that surrounds you, offering a break from the chains that bind you to your desk and smart phone.

This tiny tome is your trusty companion – campanion, if you will – celebrating all things camping-related. It's action-packed with all the essential fun-size facts and stats, quips and tips, quotes and notes, you'll need to survive and thrive in the often frightening company of the wild. (The paper of this book, just FYI, is also specially treated to wipe your bottom safely should you forget to pack toilet paper. Just watch out for the sharp edges.)

So, pack your tent (and the instructions on how to pitch it), grab your bear/mosquito/body spray, because you're going to need all three, and let's carry on camping together! Next stop, nature… here we come!

CHAPTER
**ONE**

# Happy Campers

Hello there, happy campers! You ready to get this show on the road? We'll assume you've forgotten several of your most essential survival items and overpacked on things you're 100 per cent unlikely to ever use when camping. But's that camping! Let's get to it…

# Ten Camping Commandments

**1.** Thou shalt fart outside thy tent.

**2.** Thou shalt build thy camp before drinking thy booze.

**3.** Thou shalt not trippeth over thy guy rope.

**4.** Thou shalt only kill what wants to kill thy.

**5.** Honour thy camp neighbours.

**6.** Throweth away thy holey socks.

**7.** Thou shalt not take the Lord's name in vain, except when lost.

**8.** Thou shalt not bear false witness, except with bears.

**9.** Thou shalt covet thy partner more in thy tent (*see also* page 86).

**10.** Thou shalt not covet thy neighbour's BBQ.

# The Field of the Cloth of Gold

A diplomatic summit between England's King Henry VIII and King Francis I of France was held at two campsites on June 24, 1520. Between them, more than 2,800 tents made of a cloth of gold were used to show off their wealth. Each king tried to outdo the other, in an effort to display their power, and huge feasts, music, jousting and games occurred. King Henry, fiercely competitive, even challenged King Francis to a wrestling match. He lost.

## Things a Camper Says #1

Camping: You may lose your mind but you'll find your soul.

## Things a Camper Says #2

When it comes to camping, there's one golden rule:

Hope for the best, pack for the worst.

## Camping Hacks #1

Freeze food and drinks
before placing them in
the cool box.

**Camping Jokes #1**

Don't bother looking for
a camouflage tent
at a camping store.

You won't see any.

# S'mores

S'mores are a sweet dessert sandwich made from a piece of chocolate and a toasted marshmallow between two graham crackers. They are a tradition of US camping trips and absolutely delicious.

How you make them is simple:

**1.** Toast a marshmallow – speared with a stick – over your campfire until soft and gooey.

**2.** Squish the toasted marshmallow on a graham cracker.

**3.** Add a piece of chocolate on top.

**4.** Squish down another graham cracker.

**5.** Eat. And repeat.

\* Americans buy 90 million pounds of marshmallows each year – or half a billion marshmallows – about the same weight as 1,286 grey whales!

# Worldwide Camping Index

Rather helpfully, the esteemed Worldwide Camping Index has done a lot of camping research so we don't have to. It devised a system that worked out the best nations for camping based on criteria such as wildlife biodiversity, dangerous wildlife, stargazing, national parks, forest area, scenery, natural resources, pollution, risk of natural disaster and rainfall.

These are the top 21 nations, with all those factors considered.

1. Canada
2. Finland
3. Brazil
4. Spain
5. Sweden
6. USA
7. Australia

8. Norway
9. Argentina
10. Russia
11. Mexico
12. Costa Rica
13. Thailand
14. France

15. Japan
16. Peru
17. Tanzania
18. Croatia
19. Kenya
20. Switzerland
21. Ecuador

# Cool Camping #1: USA

According to *Time Out*, these are the top ten most beautiful campsites in the USA. What are you waiting for? Get packing…

**1**. Marin Headlands, California: Kirby Cove Campground

**2**. Assateague Island, Maryland: State Park Camping

**3**. Kapaʻa, Hawaii: Kalalau Beach

**4**. Governors Island, New York: Collective Governors Island

**5**. Grand Canyon, Arizona: North Rim

**6**. Big Sur, California: Treebones Resort

**7**. Badlands National Park, South Dakota: Sage Creek Primitive Campground

**8**. Barryville, New York: Kittatinny Campground

**9**. Catalina Island, California: Two Harbors

**10**. Florida Keys, Florida: Biscayne National Park

If you've gone deep
and dark into bear
territory, and set up
a camp, make sure
you don't pack mint-
flavoured toothpaste.
Raccoons and bears love
minty-fresh breath
and smells.

Toilet paper roll is an essential camping trip item. Before you leave home, though, take out the cardboard centre. This will make it easier to squish and pack, and will encourage you to take a spare. Trust me, you'll need it.

**66**

**April:** Andy, you have to save me. I'm camping with people I work with.

**Andy:** I don't want to be here either. The air is too fresh. It's disgusting. I can't breathe. There's a brook somewhere that won't stop babbling. Shut up!

**99**

*Parks and Recreation*, Season 3, Episode 8: "Camping"

# Bags of History

The first commercial sleeping bag was invented in 1876. Known as the "Euklisia Rug", it was patented and invented by Pryce Pryce-Jones, a Welsh entrepreneur. The Rug was made from wool and was folded and fastened at the sides. So a blanket, effectively. But what made the Rug so special was the inclusion of an inflatable rubber pillow sewn into the head of the blanket.

## Cowboy Camping

Rather romantically, sleeping under the stars without a shelter is known as "Cowboy Camping", if done on purpose.

If you've simply forgotten your tent, it's known as "uninTENTional sleeping" or "roughing it".

## The Rucksack

The first discovered rucksack — no camper leaves the home without one — dates back to around 3300 BCE. Made from animal fur, it belonged to Ötzi the Iceman, a mummy from the Copper Age, who was discovered by a group of campers at Val Senales Valley, Italy.

The word "rucksack" comes from the German zurück, meaning "back".

## Camping is good for your health.

On average, campers burn around 300 calories per hour if they are enjoying a moderately active camping trip. Way more calories than just sitting at a desk, anyway.

CHAPTER
TWO

# Nature Calls

Camping is all about reconnecting your senses with the natural world. So, see the scenery, feel the wild, taste the air, smell the earth…and hear the screams of a first-time camper who has just been told there's no Internet. Nature's calling on a landline…answer the call.

# Leave No Trace

The seven Leave No Trace principles of ethical campers, created to ensure people minimize their impact on the natural environment, are as follows:

**1**. Plan ahead and prepare

**2**. Travel and camp on durable surfaces

**3**. Dispose of waste properly

**4**. Leave what you find

**5**. Minimize campfires

**6**. Respect wildlife

**7**. Be considerate of other adventurers

**66**

Whatever form it takes,
camping is earthy, soul-
enriching and character
building, and there can be few
such satisfying moments as
having your tent pitched and
the smoke rising from your
campfire as the golden sun sets
on the horizon…

**99**

**Pippa Middleton**

## Things a Camper Says #3

Remember: camping shouldn't cost the earth, or your wallet.

# **Bear-proofing**

Keep in mind these handy tips
to avoid attracting bears.

**1**. Choose a campsite away from berry
patches or other natural food sources.

**2**. Prepare and cook food downwind of
your campsite.

**3**. Use a bear canister to keep your food
safe or make a bear bag (see page 135).

**4**. Check the area for signs of recent
activity, such as digging or bear prints.

**5**. Keep it clean. Pack away all your
rubbish and food, even the smallest bits,
and clean pots and dishes immediately
after eating.

# Camp-phobias

Camping can bring on all manner of natural phobias. Which one best describes you?

Achluophobia – a fear of darkness

Arachnophobia – a fear of spiders

Dendrophobia – a fear of trees

Entomophobia – a fear of insects

Mysophobia – a fear of dirt and germs

Noctiphobia – a fear of the night

Ombrophobia – a fear of rain

Ornithophobia – a fear of birds

Selenophobia – a fear of the moon

Trypophobia – a fear of holes

Astraphobia – a fear of thunder

Zoophobia – a fear of animals

# "She'll Be Coming 'Round the Mountain"

This popular campfire song was written in the 1890s, but do you know who the "she" refers to? It is believed, "she" is Mary Harris "Mother" Jones, a US union organizer who formed the first labour unions at the coal-mining camps in the Appalachia region during the building of the US railroad, following the abolition of slavery.

The melody is "borrowed" from a tune "When the Chariot Comes", a plantation hymn sung by African-American plantation workers.

# Pre-trip Tips

Before you pack up your kit and hit the road, make sure you do the following:

**1**. Test your gear. Make sure everything is in working order and no parts or essential items are missing.

**2**. Check the weather forecast.

**3**. Make a packing list of everything you need, and don't forget essentials like the first-aid kit, flashlights and batteries, portable chargers.

**4**. Pack your camper or car in order of what you need - the first things you want to set up, like the tent, go in last.

# Camp's the Word

The word "camp" arose in the 1520s and was used to describe a place where an army would rest and recover temporarily.

The English word derives from the French *camp*, the Italian *campo*, and from the Latin *campus* — an open field or level ground.

# Things a Camper Says #4

Camping is a lot like making love in a hammock – an unforgettable experience that can turn miserable suddenly.

# Camping Around the World

There are cool campsites all over the world. Make sure you know the word camping wherever you're heading!

Estonian — *telkimine*
Finnish — *telttailu*
Icelandic — *tjaldsvæði*
Irish — *campála*
Italian — *campeggio*
Lithuanian — *stovyklavietė*
Portuguese — *acampamento*
Scots — *campachadh*
Slovak — *kempovanie*
Spanish — *cámping*
Welsh — *gwersylla*

# *Cat Hole*

Can you guess what a cat hole is? Nope, it's not that. But you're close.

A cat hole is a camping term to mean a hole you dig to poop into, if you're wild camping. This cat hole should, obviously, be as far away as possible from your campsite. Don't poop where you camp. Mark your territory with a flag, to warn others.

Wild camping involves wild weeing. When urinating outside, try to always urinate in the same spot. And make that spot only as far as you're willing to walk from your tent at 3am in the pitch-black darkness.

Before bedtime, choose a spot and make sure the path is clear of obstructions.

# *Boondocking*

This wonderfully named term means to take your RV and camp off-the-grid, far from any amenities provided by RV parks or campgrounds.

It's the same as wild or dry camping when you've only got a tent.

Sleeping at a campsite?
Always take ear plugs.
You never know what
beasts lie at next door's
campsite. Sound travels.
That's doubly true
for snoring.

66

# I would start a revolution, but I just bought a hammock.

99

**Zach Galifianakis**

## Boy Scouts of America

Created in 1910 by Ernest Thompson Seton, the Boy Scouts of America relied heavily on camping to encourage boys to join. In its 100-year history, there have been more than

## 100 million Boy Scouts,

the largest youth organization in the world.

# Movies to Camp To

When sleeping under a canopy of sparkly stars, get out your iPad and stream these camping-related movies. Better yet, download them before you go. The Wi-Fi in nature is shocking.

The Great Outdoors (1988)
Moonrise Kingdom (2012)
Without a Paddle (2004)
RV (2006)
Meatballs (1979)
Into the Wild (2007)
Ernest Goes to Camp (1987)
A Walk in the Woods (2015)
Carry on Camping (1969)
Stand by Me (1986)

## Camping Jokes #2

Q: Why don't mummies go camping?

A: They're afraid to relax and unwind!

# Campfire Songs: Classic Rock

"Ring of Fire", Johnny Cash

"Our House", Crosby, Stills, Nash
and Young

"Brown Eyed Girl", Van Morrison

"Yellow Submarine", The Beatles

"Stand by Me", Ben E. King

"Mrs Robinson", Simon and Garfunkel

"Sweet Caroline", Neil Diamond

"Sittin' on the Dock of the Bay",
Otis Redding
"House of the Rising Sun",
The Animals

66

The man who
is blind to the
beauties of nature
has missed half the
pleasure of life.

99

**Richard Baden-Powell**

## Things a Camper Says #5

A bad day camping is still better than a good day at a desk.

66

In a well-ordered
universe, camping
would take place
indoors.

99

**Morgan Matson**

**"**

# Camping is nature's way of promoting the motel business.

**"**

**Dave Barry**

**"**

If camping is so great, why are the bugs always trying to get in your house?

**"**

**Jim Gaffigan**

## Camping Hacks #2

Put an extra blanket or duvet under your air bed, mat or sleeping bag. Coldness travels up through the ground, so the more layers between you and the ground, the warmer you'll be.

**"**

My wish is to stay
always like this,
living quietly in a
corner of nature.

**"**

**Claude Monet**

CHAPTER
**THREE**

# Tent
# Sweet Tent

Camping, of course, is not just about finding a new home away from home. It's about taking home comforts with you while camping. From tents to sleeping bags, survival kits to essential bits, there's all sorts of interesting things we think we need when wandering in the great wide yonder.

66

How is it that one match can start a forest fire, but it takes a whole box of matches to start a campfire?

99

**Christy Whitehead**

Traditional Bedouin tents, used by nomadic Arab tribes in the Middle East and North Africa, are made out of black goat hair.

The Bedouin term for tent is *buryuut hajar*, which literally means "house of hair".

**"**

# The fire is the main comfort of camp, whether in summer or winter.

**"**

**Henry David Thoreau**

# 250,000 tents

are abandoned at
music festivals across the
UK every year.

One tent is the equivalent
of leaving behind
## 250
## plastic pint cups.

**"**

It always rains on tents.
Rainstorms will travel
thousands of miles,
against prevailing winds
for the opportunity to
rain on a tent.

**"**

**Dave Barry**

**"**

Sometimes the
embers are better
than the campfire.

**"**

**Stephen King**

More than 40 million Americans go camping in the United States every year and each took an average of 3.8 trips that lasted 2.7 nights per year. They drove an average of 146 miles (235km) to get to their destinations and set up camp about ¼ mile (400m) from their cars. Approximately 42 per cent of these campers choose to camp at one of the 4,300 state park campgrounds.

There are a few types of tents in the world, from yurts to tipis.

The predecessor to today's bell tent, one of the most common used in camping, was patented by Henry Sibley in 1856 and called the Sibley tent.

Jetlagged? Go camping. Your body will reset its clock quicker thanks to the abundance of natural sunlight.

There are more than **4,800 tent campsites** in the UK. Cornwall has the most. During the COVID-19 pandemic, Cornwall became the UK's most visited county, up 20 per cent over their average 5 million per year.

Did you know one of the
first recorded mentions of
a tent is in the *Bible*?

**66**

Adah gave birth to Jabal;
he was the father of
those who live in tents
and raise livestock.

**99**

**Genesis 4:20**

According to a 2020 survey, 38 per cent of people in the United States and Canada consider themselves life-long campers, and 21 per cent of Americans camped for the first time in 2020.

## Camping Jokes #3

Q: What do you call a bunch of crows out for camping?

A: Murder within tent

Today's tents are all about being super-ultra lightweight.

The lightest tent available to buy on the market is currently the Laser Pulse Ultra 1. It weighs just 1 pound (450g) – the same weight as a FIFA regulation football.

The 2021 North American Camping Report found that the number of households who went camping grew by 3.9 million households in 2020 – the largest spike since the report began.

**66**

Now I see the secret of making the best person: it is to grow in the open air and to eat and sleep with the earth.

**99**

**Walt Whitman**

A flashlight (or torch) is considered the most essential camping gear after a tent, and, yet, it's the last thing we remember to pack when we go camping. But did you know that the first flashlight was invented by David Misell, an English inventor, in 1899?

They were called "flash" lights because they could not throw light for too long and you had to turn them off to "rest" the batteries.

## Things a Camper Says #6

If it starts to cloud when camping, don't worry — every tent has a silver lining.

## Things a Camper Says #7

Camping is great for when you're craving a horrible night's sleep.

## Camping Hacks #3

Never, ever, ever, ever, push your tent pegs using your feet. They'll bend straight away and become useless. Always use a mallet. You'll thank me when it comes time to pack your tent.

## Things a Camper Says #8

Time spent camping
is not spent, it's
invested.

# Camp-acronym

The seven-letter word camping, as an acronym, also spells out the seven best things about camping.

**C**ampfires

**A**dventure

**M**arshmallows

**P**uddles

**I**nsects

**N**ature

**G**etaway

Between 2020 and 2021, a record number (16,608) of new motorhomes were registered in the UK, totalling sales of £1.15 billion (about US$1.56 billion), according to the National Caravan Council.

The king of all campervans, the Volkswagen California, also enjoyed a 621 per cent year-on-year rise, not including an exploding second-hand market.

## Things a Camper Says #9

Good things come to those who camp.

Items campers consider
to be the most essential are:

**Tent** (61%)

**Sleeping bag** (38%)

**Bug spray** (24%)

**Cooler** (23%)

**Firewood** (22%)

In 2019, the last year data was available, UK campers went on more than 9.3 million trips, spending £2.2 billion (almost US$3 billion).

There are an estimated 1.2 million regular campers in the UK.

# Stargazing

According to the Worldwide Camping Index, these are the planet's best places to look at the night sky and see nothing but stars.

*Light pollution by percentage*

| | |
|---|---|
| Mongolia – 0.1 | Nepal – 1.2 |
| Tanzania – 0.2 | Peru – 1.7 |
| Kenya – 0.7 | Canada – 2.7 |
| Zimbabwe – 0.7 | Kazakhstan – 2.9 |
| Australia – 0.9 | Russia – 4.9 |

*For context, England has 78.3 per cent light pollution.

Campervan and caravan camping has become the cool kid on the holiday block, following the COVID-19 pandemic. It's also the environmentally friendly choice.

As opposed to travelling by plane, a family of four, on average, saves 8.6 hours of travel time, spends 92 per cent less on transport costs, and reduces their $CO_2$ emissions by 95 per cent – enough to brew 80,472 cups of tea!

## Things a Camper Says #10

Campers love to beat around the bush.

Men account for nearly 75 per cent of camping deaths at US national parks. Heart attacks are the most common cause.

Thanks, hiking.

According to a 2015 study by tent manufacturer Olpro, married people are more likely to have more sex while camping than at home, citing 45 per cent less distractions and that being in the great outdoors is a big turn-on.

Wonderfully, Olpro have seen tent sales increase by 50 per cent since the study.

**66**

I am a happy camper so I guess I'm doing something right. Happiness is like a butterfly; the more you chase it, the more it will elude you, but if you turn your attention to other things, it will come and sit softly on your shoulder.

**99**

**Henry David Thoreau**

**"**

Camping is pointless. You take a bath and dress up to drive hours to a place with no showers or laundry.

**"**

**Homer Simpson, *The Simpsons*,
Season 26, Episode 7: "Blazed and Confused"**

**66**

If we walk in the woods, we must feed mosquitoes.

**99**

**Ralph Waldo Emerson**

66

The man who goes
afoot, prepared to camp
anywhere and in any
weather, is the most
independent fellow
on earth.

99

**Horace Kephart**

The actual name of the Swiss Army knife is the "Swiss Officers and Sports Knife", or *Schweizer Offiziers und Sportmesser*.

During World War II, American soldiers become besotted with these nifty little knives and brought them home to America. People there had trouble pronouncing the German name and simply referred to them as Swiss Army knives.

The knives issued to the Swiss Military are not the iconic red colour; they are aluminium.

**❝**

The echoes of beauty
you've seen transpire,
Resound through dying
coals of a campfire.

**❞**

**Ernest Hemingway**

Tents are like
secrets. Once
they're out the
bag, their bloody
difficult to get
back in again.

CHAPTER
**FOUR**

# The Great Outdoors

Unlike many things in modern life that are actually anti-climactic when viewed up close and intimate, the Great Outdoors never disappoints. How can it? It has everything you'll ever need to recharge your batteries... without needing a password.

In August 1907, Lieutenant-General Robert Baden-Powell organized a camp for boys at Brownsea Island, Poole Harbour. Powell used the camp to test his ideas for his book, *Scouting for Boys*. The camp invited boys from all sorts of British social backgrounds to attend and participate in activities around camping.

The camp was a huge success. It encouraged Baden-Powell to found the Scout movement, making the Brownsea Island camp the first-ever Scout camp.

Camping at a festival? Make your tent stand out from the crowd so you can recognize it when returning home later and "tired and emotional". A flag on a pole above your tent is best, as you can see it from far away.

# S-P-U-D

Is this the best camping game?
We think so. All you'll need is a tennis ball,
so make sure you pack one.
Here are the rules:

**1**. Choose one player for the centre.

**2**. The rest of the players form a circle
and are assigned a number.

**3**. The player in the middle shouts
out someone's number and throws the
ball straight up.

**4**. The camper whose number
was called must catch the ball.
Everyone else starts running away
from the centre.

**5**. Once the camper has caught the ball, they yell "SPUD!" (or whatever word you want) and everyone else freezes.

**6**. That player can then take three steps toward any of the players and throw the ball at them.

**7**. The player can dodge the ball, but must not move their feet.

**8**. If hit, the player takes an "S". If the thrower misses, the thrower takes an "S".

**9**. Once a player reaches "S-P-U-D", they're out.

**10**. The last one out wins — and dishes out punishment to the rest of the players.

# Camping Movies: Horror

According to Hollywood, camping in the woods with a group of friends is a sure-fire way to meet a gruesome and grisly death… usually at the hands of a slasher. Watch these films if you dare!

**1**. The Cabin in the Woods (2011)
**2**. Cabin Fever (2002)
**3**. Friday the 13th, Part 2 (1981)
**4**. Wrong Turn (2003)
**5**. The Burning (1981)
**6**. Wolf Creek (2005)
**7**. Blair Witch Project (1999)
**8**. The Evil Dead (1981)
**9**. Eden Lake (2008)
**10**. Madman (1981)

# Dangerous Wildlife

According to the Worldwide Camping Index, the nations with the most dangerous species – just in case it influences your camping trip decision – are as follows.

| | |
|---|---|
| **1**. Mexico | **6**. Colombia |
| **2**. Brazil | **7**. Vietnam |
| **3**. Australia | **8**. Thailand |
| **4**. India | **9**. Peru |
| **5**. Indonesia | **10**. Ecuador |

## Things a Camper Says #11

Camping – if you ain't drunk, you're doing it wrong.

**66**

If people sat outside and looked at the stars each night, I'll bet they'd live a lot differently.

**99**

**Bill Watterson**

**❝**

Camping is not a date;
it's an endurance test.
If you can survive
camping with someone,
you should marry them
on the way home.

**❞**

**Yvonne Prinz**

**66**

# Remember: If it's too hot to touch, it's too hot to leave.

**99**

US Forestry Service advice on campfires

**"**

Earth and sky, woods and fields, lakes and rivers, the mountain and the sea, are excellent schoolmasters, and teach of us more than we can ever learn from books.

**"**

**John Lubbock**

## Camping Hacks #4

Take as many solar-powered stake lights and lamps as possible. Mark out your campsite and guy ropes with stake lights, and suspend a light from a tree above your cat hole so you can, quite literally, see where you're going.

## Things a Camper Says #12

Saving for a rainy day?
Go camping.

In the UK, the average
cost of camping for
2.73 nights is
£186 (US$253) for
3.29 people. The average
price cost of glamping
is more than double
at £481 (US$654).

The outdoor accommodation specialist, Pitchup.com, which offers campers access to over 6,000 campsites in the EU and across the US, has reported a 500 per cent spike in bookings from the UK for July and August 2021.

In the UK, campsite bookings have also increased by 500 per cent for some parts of the country, according to the Cool Camping travel agency.

According to a study in 2017, the importance of campers having access to an Internet connection has decreased from 37 per cent to 29 per cent.

Are we finally learning to disconnect?

For UK campers, breakfast is the most important meal of the day, with more than 44 per cent of the online social media chat. Lunch is second most important, at 30 per cent, and dinner last, with 26 per cent. Bacon and eggs is the most popular camping breakfast.

# Forest Areas

According to the Worldwide Camping Index, these are the top ten countries with the highest amount of forested area.

*Forest area by percentage*

| | |
|---|---|
| Finland – 73.1 | Slovenia – 62 |
| Sweden – 68.9 | Panama – 61.9 |
| Japan – 68.5 | Brazil – 58.9 |
| Malaysia – 67.6 | Peru – 57.7 |
| South Korea – 63.4 | Costa Rica – 54.6 |

*For context, England is 10 per cent forested.

# Cool Camping #2: UK

According to *Time Out*, these are the top 12 most beautiful campsites in the UK.

Where are you going next?

1. Cornish Tipi Holidays, Bodmin
2. Eye Kettleby Lakes, Chichester
3. Kilvrecht Campsite, Perthshire
4. Ten Acres Vineyard, Winkleigh
5. Trwyn yr Wylfa Camping Site, Penmaenmawr
6. Carrowmena Activity Centre, Limavady
7. Fidden Farm, Fionnphort
8. Low Wray Campsite, Ambleside
9. Castle Knights, Usk Castle
10. Hooks House Farm, Robin Hoods Bay
11. Top of the Woods, Boncath
12. Invercaimbe Campsite, Invercaimbe

# Mosquito-no-no

Mosquitos and midges love to go to camping too – specifically with you and at your campsite. They can cause a cool camping trip to turn into a massacre.

Fend them off with the following:

**1**. Coffee grounds – rub them over your body*

**2**. Citronella candles

**3**. Garlic

**4**. Sulfur

**5**. Lavender

**6**. Rosemary

**7**. Apple cider vinegar

**8**. Fire

*Just kidding. Scatter them around your site.

In the US in 2020,
55 per cent of first-time
campers went camping
as a direct result of
concerns surrounding
COVID-19 and being
near other people.

**“**

"All over America today people would be dragging themselves to work, stuck in traffic jams, wreathed in exhaust smoke. I was going for a walk in the woods. "

**”**

**Bill Bryson**

**66**

**Ben:** I don't really go camping, ever, so I'm not gonna spend $150 on a tent. I'm just gonna sleep on the floor.

**Ron Swanson:** It's called the ground when it's outside.

**99**

*Parks and Recreation*, Season 3, Episode 8: "Camping"

# *Glamping*

This word, from "glamorous camping" first appeared in the UK in 2005 and was added to the Oxford English Dictionary in 2016.

However, it is not a recent phenomenon. In the 16th century, the Earl of Atholl offered King James V a glamping experience in the Highlands, with large, pitched tents filled with all the lavish amenities and provisions from his palace at home.

**"**

# Camping isn't really a vacation, but it sure makes for good memories.

**"**

**Julie Kieras**

There are now more than 13 million households in the US with an RV. Luckily, there's more than

**16,000 campgrounds**

they can go to jack in.

Unless they're boondockers (see page 40).

# Pollution

According to the Worldwide Camping Index, these nations enjoy the least amount of pollution.

Will this sway your decision?

1. Finland
2. Sweden
3. Estonia
4. Norway
5. Denmark
6. Switzerland
7. Australia
8. Slovenia
9. Canada
10. Germany

Sleeping in a tent is one of two things – boiling hot* or freezing.

To prevent the latter, heat a large flat stone at the base of your campfire to the same temperature as hot bath water – 105°F (40°C), or so. Use tongs to pick it up.

Then, wrap the stone in a cloth or towel and put it in your sleeping bag an hour before you plan to go to bed. You'll be toasty and warm for hours!

*If you're hot, either unzip the tent or pack a travel fan to circulate the humid air.

> **"**
>
> # A walk in nature walks the soul back home.
>
> **"**
>
> **Mary Davis**

"

Take nothing but pictures, leave nothing but footprints, kill nothing but time.

"

**Aliyyah Eniath**

Cooking on hot coals over
the campfire?

Don't burn your burger.
Place your hand 4 inches (about
10cm or four fingers' width)
above the coals — if you can
hold your hand there for no
more than two seconds, you're
ready to BBQ.

If in doubt, only put your meat
on coals that glow orange.
Nothing more.

**"**

Cooking and eating
food outdoors makes it
taste infinitely better
than the same meal
prepared and
consumed indoors.

**"**

**Fennel Hudson**

## Camping Jokes #4

Q. Why is camping so stressful?

A. It's in tents.

The most popular US pastime while camping is hiking — with 46 per cent of campers putting their boots on.

54 per cent of all
US campers travel
less than 100 miles
from home
to their camping
destination.

60 per cent of campers
ues tents and it is
the primary type of
accommodation.

CHAPTER
**FIVE**

# Keep Calm and Camp On

There's never a dull moment when camping — there's a fun fact to be learned under every rock, up every tree and in every tent. From survival tips to handy hints, what you learn today may just save a life tomorrow. Or, more likely, impress your friends around a campfire. But still, a lesson learned is a burger earned, as campers like to say.

## Bear Bag

If you're setting up camp deep in bear territory, don't forget to make your own bear bag. Put your food in a waterproof bag and then attach it to a rope. Suspend the bag over a tree branch out of reach of a bear's grasp, and tie the rope around the tree. This will protect your food from bears or any large mammals nearby who might wander into your camp looking for a decent meal.

# *Hula Skirt*

This is a brush-like mud guard that attaches to the rear bumper of an RV to prevent the debris and stones kicking up from the road from hitting the tow or vehicle behind you. Also called a "dirt skirt".

When choosing a campsite away from campgrounds or out in the wilderness, select a flat, open area with low or no grass – to keep snakes away.

An open area will also protect you should an animal wander in – it can run off without feeling enclosed and becoming aggressive.

"

Once all the power goes
out, there will still be
human beings standing
together around a
campfire, playing
acoustic guitars.

"

**Jim James**

# Cool Camping #3: Europe

According to *The Guardian*, these
20 campsites in Europe are above and beyond
beautiful – they're the best.

Check them out!

**1**. Le Clos du Lac, Provence, France

**2**. Le Chant-hibou, Auvergne, France

**3**. Camping La Pointe, Brittany, France

**4**. D'Olde Kamp, Ansen, Netherlands

**5**. Landgoed de Barendonk, Beers, Netherlands

**6**. Camping de la Cascade, Coo, Belgium

**7**. Zur Mühle, Black Forest, Germany

8. Camping Mexico, Bregenz, Austria

9. Camping Lindenhof, Bern, Switzerland

10. Camping Val d'Or, Enscherange, Luxembourg

11. Camping Carso, Trieste, Italy

12. Camping Camino de Santiago, Burgos, Spain

13. Campsite Port Massaluca, Catalonia, Spain

14. Quinta dos Moinhos, Braga, Portugal

15. Campsite Nature Ferie, Hals, Denmark

16. Fyrväpplingen Fiskecamp, Uppsala, Sweden

17. Camp Vala, Mokalo, Croatia

18. Camp Liza, Bovec, Slovenia

19. Camp 9 Nature Campground, Silesia, Poland

20. Tartaruga Camping, Zakynthos, Greece

If camping wild, don't camp where you cook. Experts suggest you pitch your tent, or campsite, around 200 feet (60m) from where you cook. You know why.

# Risk of Natural Disaster

According to the Worldwide Camping Index, these nations are the least at risk of natural disaster. Hold on to your hats...

*Risk of natural disaster by percentage*

Sweden – 2.12 | France – 2.62
Norway – 2.19 | Oman – 2.64
Finland – 2.21 | Denmark – 2.89
Estonia – 2.36 | Lithuania – 2.92
Switzerland – 2.37 | Germany – 2.95

The very first
commercial campground
in the world was – so historians
think – Cunningham's Camp
in Douglas, on the Isle of Man.

It opened in 1894.

66

Some national parks
have long waiting lists
for camping reservations.
When you have to wait
a year to sleep next to a
tree, something is wrong.

99

**George Carlin**

**"**

The outside is
the only place
we can truly be
inside the world.

**"**

**Daniel J. Rice**

## Things a Camper Says #13

Camping — the only rational answer for leaving a warm house with solid walls to sleep on the cold ground.

**66**

# Better to have him inside the tent pissing out, than outside the tent pissing in.

**99**

**President Lyndon B. Johnson**

## Camping Hacks #5

Tuck the bottom of your trouser legs into your socks to prevent insects, bugs and poisonous snakes* from climbing inside your trousers.

*Just kidding about the snakes.

## Things a Camper Says #14

A campfire is more than just a fire – it's nature's nightclub.

**66**

I married a woman who
loves to camp, and I am what
you would call indoorsy…
My wife always brings up,
camping's a tradition in my
family. Hey, it was a tradition
in everyone's family 'til we
came up with the house.

**99**

**Jim Gaffigan**

**"**

I got into an argument with
a girlfriend inside of a tent.
That's a bad place for an
argument, because then I tried
to walk out and slammed the
flap. How are you supposed
to express your anger in this
situation? Zipper it up
really quick?

**"**

**Mitch Hedberg**

According to the
Guinness Book of World
Records, the fastest time
to set up a campsite, by a
team of two, is

**74.48 seconds.**

This feat was achieved
by Duoduo Wang and
Lester Liu in Shanghai,
China, on July 24, 2020.
Can you beat it?

**66**

# A week of camp life is worth six months of theoretical teaching in the meeting room.

**99**

**Robert Baden-Powell**

# *Billy Can*

A small metal container with
a handle at the top used to
boil water or cook food over a
campfire. Originally used in the
Australian Outback, where
to "boil the billy" means to
make tea.

# Cool Camping #4: The World

According to *Rough Guides*, these are the best places in the world to pitch your tent and breathe in the breath-taking views.
If you want to know why, you'll have to find out for yourself!

**1**. Mount Cook National Park, New Zealand

**2**. Dartmoor and Exmoor, Devon, England

**3**. Loch Lomond and the Trossachs, Scotland

**4**. The Alps, France

**5**. Hossa National Park, Finland

6. Skåne, Sweden

7. Zion National Park, Utah, USA

8. Vancouver Island, British Columbia

9. Patagonia, Argentina and Chile

10. Asturias, Spain

11. Connemara, Ireland

12. Simien Mountains, Ethiopia

13. Tasmania, Australia

14. The Seto Inland Sea
(Setonaikal), Japan

15. Ladakh, India

# Rainfall

According to the Worldwide Camping Index, these ten countries stay drier than the other 190 nation states. For many campers, this information will be invaluable.

## Amount of rain (in inches)

| | |
|---|---|
| Oman – 3.8 | Russia – 20.1 |
| Mongolia – 9.3 | Spain – 21.7 |
| Kazakhstan – 11.6 | Finland – 21.9 |
| Morocco – 16.9 | Sweden – 22.6 |
| Ukraine – 20.1 | Latvia – 23.2 |

*For context, England receives 33.7 inches of rainfall a year.

If you're camping and want to know the temperature, but aren't connected to the Internet, don't panic, nature's got your back. During the spring and summer months, you can calculate the temperature by listening to a chirping cricket. Simply count the number of chirps you hear in 14 seconds. Then, add 40 to that number to find out the temperature in degrees Fahrenheit.

CHAPTER
**SIX**

# Sticks and Stones

We've reached the end of our camping trip. It's almost time to go back to the real world and leave the natural one behind — until next time. But before we head in from the hike, let's take one last trip around the campsite and make sure we've not left anything behind. Because, remember, when it comes to camping rule number one is…leave no trace.

**"**

A great many people,
and more all the time,
live their entire lives
without ever once
sleeping out under
the stars.

**"**

**Alan S. Kesselheim**

**66**

The wilderness
holds answers to
questions we have not
yet learned to ask.

**99**

**Nancy Wynne Newhall**

**"**

# Light a campfire and everyone's a storyteller.

**"**

**John J. Geddes**

If you're building a campfire to stay warm, cedar is the best wood to use. It won't produce as large a flame as birch or oak, but it packs a bigger punch when it comes to sustained heat.

66

# Life is simple.
# Eat.
# Sleep.
# Camp.

99

**Anon**

66

I just want to live in a world of mountains, coffee, campfires, cabins and golden trees, and run around with a camera and notebook, learning the inner workings of everything real.

99

**Victoria Erickson**

## Things a Camper Says #15

What happens at camp, stays at camp.

66

My tent doesn't look like much but, as an estate agent might say, it is air-conditioned and has exceptional location.

99

**Fennel Hudson**

**"**

I felt my lungs
inflate with
the onrush of scenery.
Air, mountains,
trees, people.
I thought, 'This is
what it is
to be happy.'

**"**

**Sylvia Plath**

**66**

The echoes of beauty
you've seen transpire,
resound through dying
coals of a campfire.

**99**

**Ernest Hemingway**

**"**

We now no longer
camp as for a night,
but have
settled down on
earth and forgotten
heaven.

**"**

**Henry David Thoreau**

66

The stars were better
company anyway.
They were very beautiful,
and they almost
never snored.

99

**David Eddings**

**"**

What on earth would I
do if four bears came into
my camp? Why, I would
die of course. Literally
shit myself lifeless.

**"**

**Bill Bryson**

## Things a Camper Says #16

Remember: It's impossible to go for a walk in the woods and be in a bad mood at the same time.

## Things a Camper Says #17

Camping is nature's way of feeding mosquitoes.

## Camp America

In 1861 in the US, Frederick William Gunn formed the Gunnery School for Boys in Washington, Connecticut. It was the first boys' camp of its kind and boosted the popularity of recreational camping.

The first girls' camp was established in 1888. These camps kickstarted the very first summer camps for US children, which would culminate in the Camp America program.

**"**

I never saw a man who looked
With such a wistful eye
Upon that little tent of blue
Which prisoners call the sky.

**"**

**Oscar Wilde**

## Camping Hacks #6

It may not be as slimming, but when camping, opt to wear light-coloured clothing. Bugs and insects are attracted more to dark-coloured clothing.

66

Marry an outdoors woman. Then if you throw her out into the yard on a cold night, she can still survive.

99

**W. C. Fields**

Fun fact-o,
the five words most associated
with camping are:

**Fun** (84%)
**Adventure** (80%)
**Campfire** (89%)
**Tent** (83%)
**Outdoors** (89%)

**"**

# Who has smelled the woodsmoke at twilight, Who has seen the campfire burning, Who is quick to read the noises of the night?

**"**

**Rudyard Kipling**

66

The body seems to feel beauty
when exposed to it as it feels
the campfire or sunshine,
entering not by the eyes
alone, but equally through all
one's flesh like radiant heat,
making a passionate, ecstatic
pleasure glow not explainable.

99

**John Muir**

## Things a Camper Says #18

Camping only costs an arm and a leg if you piss off a bear.

# Tents of All Shapes and Sizes

In 2021, these are the top types of tents — say that ten times fast — you'll see at campsites across the UK.

What's your tent of choice?

**1**. Grass Pitch

**2**. Grass Pitch with electricity

**3**. Bell Tent

**4**. Pod

**5**. Shepherd's Hut

**6**. Woodland Pitch

**7**. Cabin

**8**. Yurt or Ger

**9**. All-Weather with electricity

**10**. Safari Tent

## Things a Camper Says #19

On your feet – lose your seat.

# Baby Boomers

While Millennials and Gen-Xers are hot on their heels in terms of camping numbers, Baby Boomers still camp the most around North America. But, what on earth, do they get up to?

Hiking – 51%

Fishing – 51%

Sight-seeing – 46%

Visit historical sites – 40%

Bird watching – 33%

Canoeing and kayaking – 31%

Biking – 25%

Backpacking – 16%

Mountain biking – 9%

Trail running – 5%

Going camping?
Forgotten your guitar?
Don't worry, someone
else will bring theirs.
Guaranteed.

Know this.
No matter where you stand.
No matter where you
move, or how far you stand
back. No matter if its windy or
not. Campfire smoke will
hunt you down, find you and
reach down inside your
lungs and haunt them.

Oh, and it'll burn itself into
your clothes forever.

# UK National Parks

The UK has some of the best national parks in the world for camping.

These were the 13 most frequented in 2020.

**1**. South Downs National Park — 2.5 millions trips in 2019!

**2**. Lake District National Park

**3**. Peak District National Park

**4**. The Broads National Park

**5**. North York Moors National Park

**6**. Snowdonia National Park

**7**. Pembrokeshire Coast National Park

**8**. Yorkshire Dales National Park

**9**. Cairngorms National Park

**10**. Brecon Beacons National Park

**11**. Exmoor National Park

**12**. Loch Lomond and the Trossachs
National Park

**13**. Dartmoor National Park

## Things a Camper Says #20

Camp big – or
go home.

# Going the Distance

Going camping doesn't mean
travelling for hours and miles,
or getting on a plane, it can
mean jumping in the car
and finding the first bit of
wilderness you can find. In
the US most camping trips
occur within 50 miles (80km)
from home with 20 per cent of
camping trips taking place more
than 200 miles (322km)
from home.

**"**

# Nature is not a place to visit. It is home.

**"**

**Gary Snyder**